The Last of the Mohicans

JAMES FENIMORE COOPER

Level 2

Retold by Coleen Degnan-Veness
Series Editors: Andy Hopkins and Jocelyn Potter

Pearson Education Limited
Edinburgh Gate, Harlow,
Essex CM20 2JE, England
and Associated Companies throughout the world.

ISBN: 978-1-4058-4287-7

First published 1826
First published by Penguin Books 1986, renewed 2000
This edition published 2008

Sixteenth impression 2022

Text copyright © Penguin Books 2000
This edition copyright © Pearson Education Ltd 2008
Illustrations copyright © David Cuzik (Pennant) 2000

Typeset by Graphicraft Ltd, Hong Kong
Set in 11/14pt Bembo
Printed in Great Britain by Ashford Colour Press Ltd.
SWTC/11

Published by Pearson Education Ltd

Every effort has been made to trace the copyright holders and we apologise in advance
for any unintentional omissions. We would be pleased to insert the appropriate
acknowledgement in any subsequent edition of this publication.

For a complete list of the titles available in the Pearson English Readers series, please
visit www.pearsonenglishreaders.com. Alternatively, write to your local Pearson Education
office or to Pearson English Readers Marketing Department, Pearson Education,
Edinburgh Gate, Harlow, Essex CM20 2JE, England.

Contents

Introduction

"My son will die one day. Then there will be nobody with Mohican blood. My son is the last of the Mohicans."

Uncas, the last of the Mohican Indians, is with his father and their white friend Hawkeye when they meet Major Heyward and the two young daughters of a British colonel. Heyward is taking the girls to their father at Fort William Henry. Magua, a Huron Indian, is also in the woods, and he hates the British. Will the girls see their father again? And can anything save the men?

James Fenimore Cooper (1789–1851) wrote his first book, *Precaution* (1820), at the age of thirty. He wanted to write better books than the English wrote at that time. Later, he wrote the six "Leatherstocking Tales," about Indians and white men. *The Last of the Mohicans* (1826) is the fifth of these six books. Hawkeye is in each story. In the other books, his name is Natty Bumpo. He cannot live with his people, so he lives in the woods with the Indians. But he is not an Indian. He is a great fighter and a good friend of the Mohicans.

In *The Last of the Mohicans*, Cooper writes about the fight between the French and the British in North America in 1757. Most of the story happens near the Hudson River and it was a wild place at that time. The story is also about the fight between white men and two Indian tribes—the Mohicans and the Hurons. Cooper wanted women to read his books, so he wrote about love, too. Some things in the story did not really happen, but that was not important. Cooper wanted his readers to enjoy a good story. He is one of America's most famous writers and this is his most famous book. There was a movie of *The Last of the Mohicans* with Daniel Day Lewis in 1992.

Chapter 1   The Trip Begins

In 1757, a lot of North America was wild country and the thick woods were often dangerous. Indians fought other Indians. Indians fought white men. The French fought the British because they wanted this country for France. Some Indians helped the British and other Indians helped the French.

The British Colonel Munro and his men were at Fort William Henry, and the Frenchman, Montcalm, and his men were near the fort. The Colonel couldn't fight Montcalm without more men, so he asked General Webb, in the north of the country, for help. Webb sent 5,000 men from Fort Edward. Colonel Munro waited for them, and he also waited for his daughters.

♦

Colonel Munro's daughters, Cora and Alice, arrived at Fort Edward from Scotland. They wanted to visit their father at Fort William Henry.

General Webb told Major Duncan Heyward, "Take the girls to their father. Don't follow the men—it's too dangerous. This Indian will show you the way."

The Indian's name was Magua.

Alice Munro looked at the Indian and his knife.

"I don't like him," she said.

"Don't be afraid. He's a friend," Major Duncan Heyward told her.

"Speak to him," said Alice. "I want to hear his English."

"He doesn't speak English, or he doesn't try," said Major Heyward.

Magua said nothing. He turned and walked away.

"Let's follow him," said Heyward to Munro's two daughters. "Only he can show us the best way to Fort William Henry."

"Cora, what do you think?" Alice asked her older sister.

But Heyward answered, "The French are more dangerous than the Indians. With Magua we will be safe from them. They don't know his way to your father's fort."

They left Fort Edward. The 1,500 men went by road, but Heyward and the two young women followed Magua through the woods.

◆

On that same day, two men sat in the woods next to the Hudson River. They talked in the language of the Mohicans. The white man wore clothes of animal skins. The other man was the Mohican Indian chief, Chingachgook.

"My tribe is the grandfather of all tribes," said Chingachgook. "The Dutch came here and they gave my people fire-water. My people were stupid and they drank it. They couldn't think. They gave our home to the Dutch. Now I am the chief, but I live in these woods. I see the sun only through the trees. I cannot visit the home of my grandfathers."

Hawkeye, the white man, listened and felt sad for his friend.

"My son will die one day. Then there will be nobody with Mohican blood," said the Indian. "My son is the last of the Mohicans."

Chapter 2   Their First Mistake

A sudden noise ended the conversation between Chingachgook and Hawkeye.

They looked up. Uncas, the chief's son, was there.

"Are there Hurons in these woods?" Chingachgook asked him.

"Yes, I think there are about ten," Uncas answered. "They are working for Montcalm and his men."

"My son is the last of the Mohicans."

Chingachgook said to Hawkeye, "We will find them and we will send them out of the woods."

Then the Indian chief put his ear to the ground and listened. He heard white men.

"Hawkeye, they are your brothers. Speak to them."

Then Hawkeye could hear them, too.

"Who's there?" he called. He put his gun across his left arm.

"We are friends. We're British," a man answered in English.

"Where are you going?" asked Hawkeye.

"To Fort William Henry. Do you know the way?" asked Major Duncan Heyward.

Hawkeye looked at Magua and laughed. "Did your Huron show you the wrong way? You want a Mohican in these woods. I can show you the right way, but it's an hour's walk from here. It will be night before that. We'll go in the morning."

Heyward looked at Magua and thought, "He's a Huron! He wants Montcalm's men and the other Hurons to find us. They'll kill us!"

Magua saw Heyward's face and understood. He shouted loudly and ran into the woods. Uncas shouted, too, and started to run after him. Suddenly, there was a loud noise. Hawkeye shot the Huron, but he didn't kill him. Magua ran away.

"We have to leave here," said Hawkeye. "That Huron will bring Montcalm's men here and they'll kill us."

Chapter 3   By Canoe up the River

"We'll help you," Hawkeye told Major Heyward. "We'll take you and the two girls up the river to Fort William Henry in our canoe."

They left the horses and walked down to the river. The canoe was under some trees.

The canoe was under some trees.

Hawkeye told them, "Sit at the front of the canoe. The Indians will go on foot."

He sat at the back, then he pushed the canoe into the Hudson River. The river was wide, fast, and dangerous, and the canoe moved very quickly. Cora and her younger sister were afraid.

"We're going to die in this river," they thought.

Then Hawkeye stopped the canoe and they got out. The two Indians were there.

"Follow us," said the Mohicans.

They took Heyward, Cora, and Alice into a cave.

Inside the cave, the two girls felt safe. The men made a fire. Major Heyward looked at Hawkeye's strange clothes and big gun. He was a very strong man. Then Heyward looked at the young Mohican. Uncas had strong arms and black eyes. He didn't have much hair—only a little on the top of his head.

Alice looked at Uncas, too. He looked kind. She said to Heyward, "I'm not afraid now because Uncas is here with us."

"Let's hope that he'll be our friend," said Heyward.

"We can eat now," said Hawkeye.

Uncas gave the girls some food. He spoke a little English to them. When he gave food to Cora, his eyes stayed on her face. He looked at her long black hair and her dark eyes. Her sister, Alice, was younger and very different. She had very light hair. Uncas liked the darker girl, Cora.

Suddenly, a Huron shouted loudly and angrily from the woods. Heyward looked at Alice. She was young, very pretty, and afraid. They heard the Indian shout again.

"Will they find us here?" the girls asked.

Then it was quiet. They listened for a long time, but there were no more sounds. The girls went to sleep. But Hawkeye and the Mohicans didn't sleep. They watched and listened.

Chapter 4   The Hurons Attack

Before morning, Hawkeye said to Major Heyward, "Wake up. We have to go. We'll go up the river in the canoe."

"Cora, Alice, wake up!" called Heyward.

Suddenly, Hurons started to shoot at them from across the river. Hawkeye shot back and killed one of the Hurons.

"They will really want us to die now," said Hawkeye.

Major Heyward said to the girls, "Follow me. You'll be safe in here."

The girls followed him to the back of the cave. It was difficult because it was dark inside.

Then Heyward went back to Hawkeye and the Mohicans. They listened, watched, and waited.

"Maybe they won't come back," said Heyward.

"You don't know the Hurons. We killed one of their men. They won't stop now," said Hawkeye.

Then they saw the heads of five Hurons in the river.

"They're coming for us," said Heyward.

But the river was fast and dangerous. There was a waterfall, and it took one of the Hurons down with it.

Then the four other Hurons climbed up the cliff above the waterfall. Hawkeye shot the nearest man.

"Take my knife! Get that one!" Hawkeye said to Uncas.

Hawkeye shot again and killed the biggest one. Heyward fought one Huron with his hands. But the Huron fought hard and Heyward was afraid. Suddenly, a dark hand with a knife cut the Indian's arm and then pulled Heyward back. The Huron fell a long way down into the river.

The four Hurons were dead. Uncas shouted happily. Then he, Heyward, and Hawkeye ran quickly behind some trees. Chingachgook was there.

Suddenly, a dark hand with a knife cut the Indian's arm and then pulled Heyward back.

Chapter 5   Cora's Plan

The Hurons across the river fired their guns, and Uncas, Chingachgook, and Hawkeye fired back.

Cora came out of the cave.

She said, "Thank you for your help, but I don't want you to die for me and my sister. Go to my father. He has to help us. He has to send more men!"

"We cannot walk away and leave two young women in this dangerous place," said Hawkeye.

But he and Chingachgook spoke in the Mohican language. Then, in English, Chingachgook said, "Yes, good."

He took his knife and tomahawk. Then he jumped into the river and started to swim away.

Hawkeye followed him.

Cora looked at Uncas and said, "Aren't you going to follow them?"

"Uncas will stay," the young Mohican answered in English.

"You have to go to my father. I want you to go," she said.

Uncas looked sadly at Cora's beautiful face. But he jumped into the river and followed his friend and his father.

Cora turned to Major Heyward. "Please go with them," she said.

Heyward looked at the beautiful Alice and she put her hand on his arm. She was young and afraid.

"I will stay," he said.

Chapter 6   War Cries

Cora, Alice, and Heyward went into the cave. They sat and talked. They began to feel happier. Then suddenly, they heard war cries. The Hurons again!

"We'll die now. They're coming nearer the cave!" said Cora.

An Indian shouted, "Hawkeye!" and then more Indians began to shout Hawkeye's name.

They hated him and they wanted to kill him. They looked for him everywhere, but they couldn't find him. Then it was strangely quiet again.

"They went away," Heyward said quietly to Cora. "Alice, we're safe!"

Alice said happily, "We'll see our father. We won't die!"

Then her face changed. Her blue eyes opened wide.

Heyward looked up and saw the angry, dark face of Magua outside of the cave. He took out his gun and fired. The noise inside the cave was very loud. There was a lot of smoke from the gun and for a minute Heyward couldn't see. Magua turned around quickly and ran away.

There was no sound in the woods for two or three minutes. Then, suddenly, loud war cries came from Magua and the other Hurons.

The Indians ran quickly into the cave and they angrily pulled the two girls and Heyward outside. Cora, Alice, and Heyward stood there with the Hurons around them. Then, the Indians smiled. They had the white man and they had the daughters of the British Colonel Munro.

Some of the Indians went back into the cave. They looked for Hawkeye, but he wasn't there.

"Where is Hawkeye?" Magua angrily asked Heyward.

Heyward answered, "He's not here."

Then suddenly, they heard war cries.

"Wait! Do not scalp her!" he said.

"Tell us. Where is he? Is he dead?" asked Magua.

"He isn't dead. He went away," answered Heyward.

"Is he a bird? Can he fly away? Or is he a fish? Can he swim up the river? The Hurons are not stupid," said Magua angrily.

"He's not a fish, but he can swim. He swam down the river, but you didn't see him," answered Heyward. Heyward was angry and not really afraid.

"Why did you stay?" Magua asked. "Do you want to lose your life?"

"A white man doesn't leave women," answered Heyward.

"And where are Chingachgook and Uncas? Did they swim down the river, too?" asked Magua.

"Yes," he answered.

The Hurons watched this conversation and waited. Then Heyward finished and Magua repeated it in their language. They shouted angrily. Then they looked with wild and angry eyes at the girls and Heyward.

Chapter 7   Magua Remembers

A dark hand suddenly pulled Alice's long hair. Heyward wanted to stop the young Indian. He pulled out his knife, but an older Indian stopped the younger man.

"Wait! Do not scalp her!" he said. He turned to Heyward and the girls. "Go!" he said.

The Indians took them down to the river, and they got into a canoe.

It was again a dangerous trip down the fast river, but the Hurons knew the river well. Then they got out of the canoe and walked for a long time through the thick woods. At night they stopped. A young Huron killed an animal and they sat down and ate.

Then Magua said to Heyward, "Go to the girl with dark hair. I want to speak to her. Bring her here."

Heyward brought Cora to him and then left her.

She asked, "What does the Huron want to say?" She looked strong and not afraid of the great fighter.

Magua took her arm, but she pulled it away.

"I was born a chief in the Huron tribe," he said. "I did not see a white man before I was twenty years old. Then the white man came. He gave me fire-water. It made me stupid. The Hurons did not want me in their tribe, so I went south through the woods. This Huron chief had to go and live with a different tribe," he said angrily. "Your people did this to me!"

"So, you hate me, too?" she asked quietly.

"No," he answered, "you are different."

"Then what do you want?" she asked.

"Later, I fought for the British. I worked for your father. Then again, white men gave me fire-water. Again I was stupid. I was not Magua. The fire-water spoke, not me. Munro, your father, was angry and, in front of his men, he hit me many times."

Cora said nothing.

"See!" said Magua, and he showed her his back. "A Huron does not forget."

She didn't look away from his back, but she slowly closed her eyes—she felt sick.

Cora said quietly, "An Indian can forget. You can be a good man. Take me and my sister to our father."

"No," answered Magua.

"What do you want?" she asked.

"I want good for good and bad for bad," said Magua with a smile.

"You will kill us because my father hit you? Take me, but not my sister. Kill only me."

"No," said Magua. "Come with me. Live with me and be my wife."

Cora's eyes opened wide.

"But, why? You don't love me. You don't want a white woman," she said.

"I want you to cook for me and to bring my water. I want you to work in my home. Munro will sleep with his guns. His daughter will sleep with me."

Cora was very angry.

"You're an animal!" she shouted at him.

He smiled and walked away to the other Indians. Cora walked back to Alice and Heyward. She was angry and unhappy.

"What did he want?" asked Heyward.

"Tell us," said Alice.

Cora put her arms around Alice and said, "Wait and see."

Magua spoke to the Hurons about white men and the home of their grandfathers. He spoke of the great fighters of his tribe and of Hawkeye. Hawkeye's gun killed some of their great fighters, so he talked about the wives and children of those men. Magua's heart was full of hate and his tribe felt this hate also.

"We will scalp more white men!" they shouted.

They were excited and angry and they wanted to kill. They pulled out their knives and tomahawks and ran to Heyward, Cora, and Alice. Heyward quickly jumped in front of the girls. He wanted to stop the Indians, but they pulled him away.

Chapter 8   Ready to Die

Magua shouted, "Do not scalp him. Make a fire! We will put them in it!"

The Indians broke wood from the trees. They were excited.

Magua looked at the daughters of Colonel Munro. Alice looked to Heyward for help. Heyward looked at her, but he couldn't save her.

"The daughter of Munro is better than me? She does not want to live with me? She wants to die?" Magua said quietly to Cora.

"What does he mean?" asked Heyward angrily.

"Nothing," answered Cora. "He's an animal."

Magua said to Cora, "I can send the younger girl to her father. Will you follow Magua? Look! The young girl is crying. She does not want to die! Send her to her father."

"What did he say?" asked Alice. "Can I go to Father?"

"You and Heyward can go to Father. But I ... I have to go with him! I have to be his wife! What can I do, Alice? Heyward, please tell me," Cora shouted.

"You will not go with Magua!" shouted Heyward.

"What do you think, Alice?" Cora asked her sister.

There was no answer. Alice was quiet.

Then she shouted, "We will die!"

"Then die!" shouted Magua.

He threw his tomahawk and it cut off some of Alice's yellow hair. But it stopped in the tree above her head. Her hair fell to the ground.

An Indian held up his tomahawk. He wanted to scalp Alice. Heyward jumped on him and they fell. The Indian was on top of Heyward and his tomahawk was ready. Suddenly, there was a loud noise from a gun. The Indian's eyes opened wildly and he fell dead on the ground next to Heyward.

Chapter 9   The End is Near

Uncas, Chingachgook, and Hawkeye ran out from behind the trees and attacked the Hurons. They, with Heyward, fought hard. They killed five men with their knives and tomahawks. Then Uncas and Magua fought, and Uncas's knife cut the Huron. Magua fell.

"He's dead!" said Hawkeye.

Uncas, Chingachgook, and Hawkeye ran out from behind the trees and attacked the Hurons.

But suddenly, Magua jumped up and ran into the woods.

"He's only one man—he can go. We won't stop him now," said Hawkeye.

"You saved us," the two girls cried. "Thank you, thank you!"

Uncas and Heyward looked at the two sisters and they felt happy.

"How did you find us?" Heyward asked Hawkeye, a little later.

"We didn't go a long way down the river. We couldn't leave you, so we watched from across the river."

"Did you see everything?" asked Heyward.

"No, but we heard," answered Hawkeye. "We have to go north now. We have to find Fort William Henry. Let's go! It's dangerous here and more Hurons will come."

Heyward, Alice, Cora, Hawkeye, Chingachgook, and Uncas went quickly through the woods. The sisters were very quiet and afraid. Everybody was tired, but they got to the top of the mountain and looked down. From there they saw Fort William Henry, and across the river were Montcalm's men—about 10,000 of them.

"There's your father's fort," said Hawkeye.

"Let's go to him!" said Cora.

"You aren't afraid to die?" asked Hawkeye. "The French and the Hurons will kill us."

They went slowly down the mountain. The weather was very bad and they couldn't see much.

At the bottom of the mountain, they stopped. Hawkeye and the Mohicans left the woods and looked around. They came back quickly.

"We can't walk through there," said Hawkeye.

"Can we walk around them?" asked Heyward.

"I think we can. Let's go," answered Hawkeye.

Suddenly, somebody shouted in French, "Who's there? Stop!" and guns fired at them.

Hawkeye fired back and the French shot again. Men shouted in French. Indians shouted too.

"Run to the fort!" shouted Hawkeye.

Uncas took Cora's arm, and they ran to the fort. The French ran after them.

Then suddenly, they heard a shout, "Wait! Fire when you can see!" It was Colonel Munro!

"Father, Father! It is me—Alice! Save your daughters!"

"Wait! Is that really my daughter?" asked Munro.

His daughters ran to him. The old Colonel put his arms around them and cried.

Chapter 10   Win or Lose

For five days the French attacked the British at Fort William Henry. General Webb's men didn't come. It was too dangerous. Hawkeye went to Fort Edward and spoke to General Webb. But Colonel Munro's men had to fight without them.

Hawkeye's trip back to Fort William Henry from Fort Edward ended suddenly when the French caught him. He had with him a letter from General Webb for Colonel Munro, and the French took it from him.

On the fifth day, Major Heyward went to Colonel Munro.

"It's very dangerous here and our men are tired," he told the Colonel.

Colonel Munro said, "Montcalm wants to talk to me, but I'm going to send you in my place."

So the fighting stopped and Major Heyward went to meet Montcalm. The Frenchman was with three of his men and the chiefs of some Indian tribes. Heyward stopped suddenly when he saw Magua. But then he turned to Montcalm.

"Let's talk," said Montcalm in French, "but I do not speak English."

"I speak a little French," said Major Heyward.

"Good. Your men fight well, but they are very tired," said Montcalm. "I understand that Munro's two daughters are in the fort now."

"They're not afraid. The older daughter can fight, too," said Heyward.

"I have more men than you. I have these Indians and they want to attack the British. Don't you want to save lives now?"

"We have more men than you think," answered Heyward.

He wanted to know about General Webb's letter, so he asked Montcalm some questions. But Montcalm didn't tell him anything. The two men said goodbye, and Major Heyward went back to the fort.

Chapter 11   A Father's Story

Colonel Munro was with his daughters.

"Major Heyward!" said Alice, happily.

"Pretty young women in this fort! What will happen next!" laughed the happy father. "Go outside, girls. The men have to talk."

When the girls left, Colonel Munro said, "They're very good girls."

"Yes, they are, sir," answered Heyward. He was happy because Munro liked him. But he wanted to talk about Montcalm.

"Montcalm said . . . ," he began.

"That Frenchman and his men can go to . . . ," Munro stopped. "He's not the Colonel of Fort William Henry, and he never will be! Webb and his men will arrive and we'll win!" he said loudly. Then, the older man changed the conversation. "Your parents and I are old friends. When I see you look at my daughters, I know a young man's heart."

"Your daughters are wonderful young women, sir. I would like to marry one of them," answered Heyward.

"I would like to marry one of them," answered Heyward.

"Cora is a very intelligent girl, and . . . ," said Munro.

"Cora?" said Heyward, "I . . . I . . ."

"Aren't we talking about Cora?" asked Munro.

"No, sir, I'm talking about your other daughter!"

"Alice?" asked Munro.

"Yes, sir."

Munro walked up and down the room for some minutes. Then he said, "Sit down and I'll tell you about my life."

Heyward sat down.

"I was a young man, too. I loved a young woman, and I wanted to marry her. But her father said no, so I left Scotland. I fought for my country in other places. I went to the West Indies and I married a woman there. She was Cora's mother. Cora's grandfather was rich, but his wife's family had no money. They worked for rich people and they worked hard. Many white people, many British people, dislike these people. It makes a father angry! And do you too think that Cora is different? Do you dislike the color of her skin?" asked Munro.

"I'm sorry, sir, but . . . ," said the young man. He looked down at the floor.

"Your blood is too good for her blood? My daughter is a good woman!" said Munro angrily.

"But Alice is a good woman too, sir."

"Yes, you're right," said the old man. "When I look at her, I remember her mother. My wife died, and I went back to Scotland. There I met the first woman again. It was twenty years later. She waited twenty years, and then she married me. She was Alice's mother. But after Alice was born, her mother died," said Munro. His face looked very old and very sad.

After a minute or two, he stood up and his face changed. "What did Montcalm say to you?"

"He wants to meet you, sir," answered Major Heyward.

"Go to Montcalm, Heyward. Colonel Munro will meet him. Tell him that. But speak to the men, Heyward. They'll have to watch and be ready. We have to be very careful with the French," said the Colonel.

Chapter 12 The Fight Ends

Montcalm and Munro met. Montcalm spoke first.

"Good day," said the Frenchman. "I will speak in French because Major Heyward can speak French and English."

Montcalm looked at his men. They came closer to him. Munro and Heyward saw the dark faces of Indians in the woods.

Montcalm started, "We can fight you and kill you. Or we can stop now. I have many men."

"Yes, you have many men," said Munro, "but we have many men, too."

"But they aren't here," answered Montcalm.

He gave Munro General Webb's letter and Munro read it. His face changed suddenly.

The letter said, "I cannot send any men to you. Give Fort William Henry to the French."

Montcalm said, "You have to go. Take your men and guns. Take everything back to England. Write your name on this paper, and then we won't fight again. The French and the British will be friends."

Munro and Montcalm wrote their names on the paper. Then, the old Colonel went back to his fort.

Sadly, he told his men, "We have to leave Fort William Henry in the morning."

The next morning, Munro and his men left the fort. There were 3,000 men, but they were quiet. Some were sick and they walked slowly behind the other men. There were some women and children and they walked behind the sick men. Munro looked tired and old.

"Your father wants to walk with his men," Heyward told Cora. "You and your sister have to go on the horses."

"I'll walk," Cora said.

"But Alice isn't as strong as you, Cora," said Heyward.

"Yes, you're right," she said sadly. Her eyes were red.

"I have to walk with the men. David Gamut will go with you and Alice. You'll be safe with him," said Heyward.

David Gamut was a singer in the church and a music teacher. Cora and Alice liked him because he was a good man.

The French arrived at the fort and they quietly watched the British men, women, and children. The British walked out of the fort and down the road.

Suddenly, about 100 Indians came quietly out of the woods. Cora looked up. She saw Magua! There was hate in his eyes, but he didn't move. Then suddenly, he made the famous Indian war cry.

More than 2,000 wild and angry Indians ran out of the woods with knives and tomahawks! In minutes, hundreds of men, women, and children were dead on the ground and their blood was everywhere. Some Indians drank it.

The British fought back, but the attack was very sudden. Munro quickly got on a horse because he wanted Montcalm. Only Montcalm could stop the Hurons.

Magua's dark eyes looked everywhere for Colonel Munro. He wanted to scalp him this time!

Munro went past his daughters on his horse.

Alice cried loudly, "Father! We're here! Come to us, Father, or we'll die!"

Munro looked at his daughters, but he couldn't stop.

Alice fell to the ground.

Gamut said, "We have to go! Come with me!"

"You can't save us," cried Cora.

Gamut began to sing. An Indian came up behind them and held up his knife. He wanted to scalp Gamut and the girls. But he heard Gamut's song and stopped.

"This man is not afraid," thought the Indian. "I will not kill him now. I will come back for him later." He ran away.

Then suddenly, Magua was there.

"Come," he said. He took Cora's arm. "You don't have to die. You can come and live with me now!"

Magua's hands were red with blood.

"I hate you!" shouted Cora.

"Magua is a great chief!" he shouted angrily. "Will you go to his tribe?"

"Never! You can kill me!" cried Cora.

Suddenly, Magua took Alice in his arms and carried her into the woods. Cora ran after Magua, and Gamut ran after her. He didn't stop singing.

The other Indians didn't stop them.

They thought, "This strange man is not really a man. He can save white women with his song."

In the woods, Cora found Magua and Alice. Magua put the two girls on a horse and Cora put her arms around Alice. Magua took them through the woods and Gamut followed. At the top of the mountain, they stopped.

"Look!" said Magua.

The girls looked down. There were about 1,500 dead men on the ground. Other men waited to die. The Hurons shouted loudly and wildly.

Gamut ran after her. He didn't stop singing.

Chapter 13   Follow and Hope

Munro went back to the place of the great fight. He was with Heyward, Hawkeye, Chingachgook, and Uncas. It was quiet now. They walked around the dead men, and they felt sick.

"Are my daughters here?" asked the Colonel.

Uncas looked at the people on the ground and found some dead women.

"Come. Look here," called Uncas. He didn't want to look. He didn't want to find Cora.

Heyward and Munro looked at the women in a pool of blood. But they didn't find Cora or Alice.

"Maybe they're not dead," they hoped.

Suddenly, Uncas called again. There was a green bag near a tree in the woods. It was Cora's bag.

"My child!" said Munro. He spoke quickly and wildly. "Give me my child!"

"Uncas will try," said the young Mohican.

Hawkeye looked at the ground.

"Uncas, look!" he said. "Cora ran into the woods. Maybe we can follow them. An Indian's eyes can see everything."

They ran as fast as they could into the woods.

"Look here, on the ground," said Uncas.

"What is it?" asked Hawkeye.

"Somebody walked here, and this was not a white man's shoe," Uncas said. He looked very carefully.

"What do you think, Uncas? Who was it?" asked Munro.

"Magua," answered Uncas.

"Magua! One day my gun will stop him," said Hawkeye angrily.

"I hope you're right," said Munro.

"Let's follow him!" said Uncas.

The great woods and mountains were wild. The Mohicans knew these woods very well, but they were dangerous. At night, the men stopped and lighted a fire. Then they slept.

In the early morning they started again. To the Mohicans, the woods were a map, and they could read every tree and every change in the ground. Hawkeye and Munro followed and watched the chief and his son.

Uncas said, "The singer has long legs. Look! He walked here."

"Were my daughters here, too?" asked Munro.

"Magua is not very intelligent, but he is not stupid," answered Uncas. "Maybe your daughters followed behind the singer, or maybe the men carried them."

They went slowly and carefully.

Then they stopped because they saw a man near a river.

Hawkeye walked to him and asked quietly, "Sir, are you teaching the animals to sing?"

"They can sing," answered Gamut.

Chapter 14   Strange Changes

"Where are the girls?" Hawkeye asked the singer quickly.

"They're with the Hurons," answered Gamut.

"Are they safe?" asked Munro.

"Yes. They're tired and unhappy, but they're well," said Gamut.

"Where's Magua?" Munro asked.

"He's in the woods. He's shooting animals for food."

"Why are you here?" Hawkeye asked.

"To the Hurons, I'm strange. I'm not a man. So, I can come and go. They don't stop me," said Gamut.

"Why don't you run away?"

"The girls are here. I have to stay here with them," answered Gamut.

"The singer has long legs. Look! He walked here."

"Go to them quietly. Give them hope. We will save them!" said their father.

"I'll go," said Gamut.

"I'll go, too," said Heyward.

"Do you want to die?" asked Hawkeye.

"I love Alice and I have to save her!"

Then Hawkeye said to Heyward, "We'll put red and blue colors on your face. The Hurons will laugh. They'll think you're funny. You can go to the girls, but be careful."

Chingachgook carefully put the colors on Heyward's face. The young man had a funny, crazy face and a big smile.

Chingachgook said, "They will not know you. Go—and do not be afraid."

"Go now," said Hawkeye, "but be careful. This is a very dangerous plan, but maybe you'll save the girls."

"I'm not afraid," said Heyward, and they left.

The Indian children saw Heyward and Gamut first. They shouted and laughed. More Indians came and looked at them. They laughed, too. The two men walked to the fires. The chiefs waited for them. They looked at Heyward carefully.

Then suddenly, there was a loud cry from the woods. Everybody ran and looked. Two Hurons came out of the woods. They held the arms of a man.

A Huron shouted something, but Heyward didn't understand it. Every Huron man, woman, and child began to shout and run wildly. They had knives and tomahawks in their hands.

The man suddenly pushed the two Hurons hard. He jumped and ran away. He ran faster than a man. A wild animal couldn't run faster. The Hurons couldn't catch him. Then the man stopped high above them, near Heyward, next to a tree. Heyward saw his face for the first time. It was Uncas!

Then one of the Hurons came from behind and quickly caught Uncas by the arm. He took him to the chiefs.

Chingachgook carefully put the colors on Heyward's face.

"You are a young Mohican, but you are a man," said an old chief with gray hair. "Two of my men are following your friend. They will catch him and bring him here."

"Do Hurons have no ears? Didn't you hear my friend's gun fire two times? Your men will never come back!" shouted Uncas.

"You can sleep tonight. Tomorrow we will speak for the last time," said the Huron chief. Then he left.

Heyward carefully went to Uncas, and said very quietly, "Where are your father and Colonel Munro?"

"They are safe. Hawkeye's gun does not sleep," said Uncas very quickly and quietly. "Go now. We cannot talk. I do not know you."

Heyward and Gamut left because they wanted to find the girls. The fires slowly died, and nobody stopped them. They suddenly saw the face of Magua, but Magua didn't see them.

Heyward and Gamut moved quietly. They found a cave and went carefully inside it. There, they saw Cora and Alice.

"It's me—Major Heyward. I'll save you!" Heyward said quietly.

The happy minute came to a sudden end when Magua stood behind Heyward and Gamut.

Then, they heard the noise of an angry animal. There was a wild animal behind Magua!

Magua looked at it and laughed. "Go away, you stupid thing! Go to the children and women. Men have to talk."

The wild animal was not really an animal. It was a man in an animal's skin and Magua knew this. Sometimes Indians wore the skins of animals, and did strange things. So Magua wasn't afraid.

Suddenly, the animal caught Magua in his strong arms. Magua couldn't move. The animal hit him on the head and he fell to the ground.

Then the man took off the animal's head and showed his face. It was Hawkeye!

Heyward, Alice, Cora, and Gamut were very happy.

"We have to go quickly!" said Hawkeye to his friends. "Put

Suddenly, the animal caught Magua in his strong arms.

Alice and Cora in these bags and we'll carry them. The Hurons won't stop us."

Heyward and Hawkeye carried the girls into the woods. There the girls got out and walked.

"Where's my friend, Uncas?" Hawkeye asked. "Can you take me to him?"

"It's very dangerous," said Gamut, "but I can."

"Wait for us. We'll come back for you," Hawkeye said to Heyward and the girls.

Uncas was in a cave. There was nobody with him.

Hawkeye, in the animal skin, and Gamut went to Uncas very quietly.

"Take this," said Hawkeye, and he gave Uncas a knife.

"Hawkeye!" said Uncas happily.

Quietly and carefully they left the cave and went back to Heyward.

Chapter 15   Love and Hate

Suddenly, they heard the loud war cry of the Hurons. The young Mohican was not in his cave, and they were very angry.

Inside the cave, Magua woke up. He wasn't dead! He ran to the Huron chief.

"They will not run away this time. Magua will find them, and they will die!" Magua shouted angrily.

The Hurons ran wildly into the woods. Hawkeye, Uncas, Heyward, Gamut, Cora, and Alice couldn't find a safe place this time. There was no hope. They could hear the Hurons. The Indians came nearer and nearer.

Suddenly, there was the dark face of Magua again. There were Hurons all around them, and this time Hawkeye didn't have his gun.

Magua took Cora's arm and pulled her away.

"She is mine!" said Magua. He looked into Uncas's eyes

He looked into Uncas's eyes and shouted, "Mohican, you know she is mine!"

and shouted, "Mohican, you know she is mine!"

"Please stop. We can give you money. Your tribe will be rich! Don't take the girl!" cried Heyward.

"Magua does not want white men's money!" the Huron shouted.

"Leave the girl," said Hawkeye. "Take me, Magua!"

Hawkeye looked at Uncas and said, "I loved you and your father. Our skins are not the same color, but we're brothers. You'll find my gun under the tree. Take it and remember me." Then he turned to Magua and said, "I'll go with you now."

"No," answered Magua. "I want the girl!" To the Hurons he said, "The other people can go. I want Cora!"

Alice cried and held Heyward's arm.

"Thank you, Hawkeye. You wanted to give your life for me. Thank you," said Cora. She looked at her sister and said to Heyward, "Love her and make her happy. She is a good person."

Cora put her arms around Alice. Then she turned to Magua and said, "Go. I will follow."

Magua and Cora walked away. The Hurons watched.

Suddenly, the great fighter, Uncas, jumped up and ran after Cora. "Stop!" he shouted.

Cora turned around and looked at him. She shouted at Magua, "I will not go with you!"

Magua looked at Uncas, then at Cora, and said angrily, "Woman, live with me or die!"

Cora looked at Uncas and cried, "I will die!"

Magua pulled out his knife, but he couldn't kill her. So another Huron ran quickly to Cora with his knife in his hand and killed her.

Uncas ran to Cora and fought Magua. Hawkeye ran to his friend, but it was too late. Uncas's blood was on Magua's knife. Uncas was on the ground, dead.

Magua looked at Hawkeye and laughed. "White men are dogs! Mohicans are women!" he shouted.

He jumped to the top of a cliff on the side of a mountain. Then he jumped again, but this time he fell. He fell off the cliff and died.

Hawkeye carried Uncas in his arms and Heyward carried Cora. Gamut helped Alice through the woods. They found Chingachgook and Colonel Munro.

Hawkeye took Chingachgook's hand and said, "I have no family. He was your son and your blood was nearer to his blood. But I will never forget my brother Uncas."

ACTIVITIES

Chapters 1–3

Before you read

1 Look at the Word List at the back of this book. Find new words in your dictionary. Then answer these questions.
   a Which are words for places?
   b Which is more important, a colonel or a major?
   c Which is more important, a colonel or a general?
   d Which is a word for a large family of American Indians?
   e Which is a word for the most important Indian?
   f Which is better, a dangerous place or a safe place?
   g Which is a word for an Indian's boat?
   h What runs from your nose when somebody hits it?

2 Look at the picture on page 3 and answer these questions.
   a Which man is the chief?
   b What is the name of his tribe?
   c What do you know about his son?

3 Read the Introduction to the book.
   a Who is a white man, Uncas or Hawkeye?
   b Why does he live in the woods with the Indians?
   c James Fenimore Cooper wrote about fights between white men and Indians. Why did he also write about love?

While you read

4 Are these sentences right? Write Yes or No.
   a The British are at Fort William Henry with Colonel Munro.   .....
   b Montcalm and his men want to fight the French.   .....
   c General Webb wants to help Colonel Munro.   .....
   d Webb sends Munro's daughters to Fort William Henry with 5,000 men.   .....
   e The Mohican tribe sold their home to the Dutch.   .....

5 Read Chapter 2. Who:
  a is Chingachgook's son? ....
  b are the Hurons working for? ....
  c has a gun? ....
  d showed Major Heyward the wrong
    way in the woods? ....
  e does Hawkeye shoot? ....
6 Read Chapter 3. What happens first? Number the sentences, 1–5.
  a The men make a fire inside the cave. .....
  b Uncas gives food to Cora and Alice. .....
  c Hawkeye takes the two young women up the
    Hudson River in a canoe. .....
  d A Huron shouts in the woods. .....
  e The Mohicans take Heyward and the sisters
    into a cave. .....

After you read

7 How do these people feel about each other? Why?
  a the Hurons and Montcalm's men
  b Heyward and Magua
  c Uncas and Cora
8 Work with another student. You are Cora and Alice. Talk about your
  day with Major Heyward and the Mohicans. Do you feel safe now?
  Why (not)?

Chapters 4–6

Before you read

9 The name of Chapter 4 is "The Hurons Attack." Discuss your
  ideas.
  a Who will they attack?
  b What will they fight with?
  c Will they kill anybody?
  d Will any Hurons die?

10 Which are the right names?

    a *Heyward/Uncas* wakes Cora and Alice.

    b *Hawkeye and Heyward/The Hurons* shoot first.

    c *Heyward/Hawkeye* takes the girls to the back of the cave.

    d *Hawkeye/Uncas* kills a Huron with a knife.

    e *The Hurons/Hawkeye and the Mohicans* win the fight.

11 Read Chapter 5. Which sentences are wrong (✗)?

    a The Hurons fire at the white men and the Mohicans. .....

    b Alice tells the men, "I don't want you to die for me and my sister." .....

    c Cora wants the men to ask her father for help. .....

    d Uncas swims away first. .....

    e Heyward doesn't follow the other men. .....

12 Read Chapter 6. Who is the speaker talking about?

    a "They're coming nearer the cave!" ....

    b "He's not a fish but he can swim." ....

    c "Did they swim down the river, too?" ....

    ....

After you read

13 Work with another student. Have this conversation.

    Student A: You are Hawkeye. Tell your friend about Major Heyward and the young women.

    Student B: You are Hawkeye's friend. Ask questions. What is Hawkeye doing? Who is he with? What is he going to do? Why?

Chapters 7–9

Before you read

14 Look at the pictures on pages 12 and 17. Who can you see? What is happening in each picture? What is going to happen between the time of the first picture and the time of the second?

15 Put a (✓) next to the important things or people in Magua's life.

    a fire-water (strong drink)   .....   **d** Colonel Munro   .....

    b the Huron tribe   .....   **e** Alice   .....

    c Major Heyward   .....   **f** Hawkeye   .....

16 What is Magua's plan in Chapter 8? Write Yes or No after each sentence.

    a He will kill Alice, Cora, and Heyward in a fire.   .....

    b He will send Alice to her father.   .....

    c He will take Cora with him.   .....

17 In Chapter 9, who says:

    a "He's only one man—he can go."   ....

    b "We couldn't leave you ..."   ....

    c "There's your father's fort."   ....

    d "Wait! Fire when you can see!"   ....

    e "Save your daughters!"   ....

After you read

18 What problems did the girls have on their way to their father? Think about the weather, the woods, the mountain, Montcalm's men, and the Hurons.

Chapters 10–12

Before you read

19 The Colonel is very happy, but Fort William Henry is a dangerous place. Why is it dangerous? What is going to happen next?

While you read

20 Who is "He" in the sentences below? Write the names.

    a He has a letter from Webb, but the French take it.   ....

    b He goes to meet Montcalm.   ....

    c He wants to marry Alice.   ....

    d He married two women.   ....

    e He gives the fort to the French.   ....

    f He takes Alice away.   ....

21 Cora and Alice are different in many ways. How are they different? Discuss the two young women.

Chapters 13–15

Before you read

22 Look at the picture on page 26.

    a Who does the Huron have in his arms?

    b What is Cora doing?

    c What do we know about this white man?

While you read

23 What happens first? Number the sentences, 1–8.

    a A Huron kills Cora. .....

    b Hawkeye and Gamut take Uncas out of the cave. .....

    c Chingachgook puts colors on Heyward's face. .....

    d Magua dies. .....

    e The Hurons catch Uncas. .....

    f Heyward and Gamut find the young women. .....

    g Magua kills Uncas. .....

    h Hawkeye hits Magua and the women get away. .....

After you read

24 Discuss these questions.

    a Who is dead at the end of the story? How did they die? Who loved them?

    b What will happen now to the Mohican tribe?

Writing

25 Write about Magua. Who was he? What happened in his life? How did he die?

26 Write a letter from Alice to a friend in Scotland after the end of the story.

27 How does Chingachgook feel after Uncas dies? What will he do now? Write about it.

28 You are General Webb. Write about Colonel Munro. What were his worst mistakes? Did *you* make any mistakes?

29 Write a conversation between Montcalm and one of his men after they arrive at Fort William Henry. How do they feel? What are they going to do next?

30 What did you learn about the Hurons and the Mohicans in this story? How are they different? Write about them.

31 Chingachgook lost his son, Hawkeye lost a "brother," Alice lost a sister, and Munro lost a daughter. Write a letter to one of these people. Tell them that you are sorry.

32 James Fenimore Cooper wrote other books about Hawkeye. Would you like to read them? Why (not)?

Answers for the Activities in this book are available from the Pearson English Readers website. A free Activity Worksheet is also available from the website. Activity worksheets are part of the Pearson English Readers Teacher Support Programme, which also includes Progress tests and Graded Reader Guidelines. For more information, please visit:
www.pearsonenglishreaders.com